SIGN LANGUAGE

SIGN LANGUAGE

Travels in Unfortunate English from
the Readers of The Telegraph

SIGN LANGUAGE

First published 2011 by
Aurum Press Limited
7 Greenland Street
London NW1 0ND
www.aurumpress.co.uk

Copyright © 2011
Telegraph Media Group

The moral right of Francisca Kellett,
Natalie Paris, Jolyon Attwooll and
Oliver Smith to be identified as the
Editors of this work has been asserted by
them in accordance with the Copyright,
Designs and Patents Act 1988.

A catalogue record for this book is
available from the British Library.

ISBN 978 1 84513 715 1

Compiled by the team at
Telegraph Travel:
Senior Editor: *Francisca Kellett*
Contributing Editors: *Oliver Smith,
Natalie Paris, Jolyon Attwooll*

10 9 8 7 6 5 4 3
2015 2014 2013 2012 2011

Design: Transmission
www.thisistransmission.com

Printed in Italy

CONTENTS

INTRODUCTION

Frankly, it's downright ungrateful. All around the world, hotel owners, shop proprietors and tourist sites do their best to make our lives easier. They translate their signs, put up helpful notices and assume, often quite rightly, that English-speaking visitors would be lost without them.

And what do we do? We point at their mistranslations. We laugh at their twisted English. We photograph their linguistic gaffes, and then, even worse, share them with the world. Although we are grateful, really. Because without those wonderful quirks of language – and our readers' desire to capture them – this book wouldn't exist.

Since the *Telegraph* first invited readers, three years ago, to send in pictures of absurd and amusing signs from their travels, we've had thousands of submissions, from the sublime ('No exit from burial site', posted outside a cemetery) to the ridiculous ('Genuine fake watches' in a Turkish shop). Many, we've noticed, have followed a number of themes, the best of which are collected here.

Those that seem to provide some of the best food for thought are the strange mistranslations found in restaurants. Some are simply bewildering, such as the 'fleshy foam' or the 'chicken of

your mother' found in eateries in China. Others might put you off your food altogether: such as an invitation to dine at the Bowels restaurant in Tokyo, perhaps, or the 'fresh crap' advertised in fish restaurants around the world. Only the strongest stomachs will fail to be put off by the 'camel dribal' advertised on a menu in Portugal, or the 'intestinal breakfast' proudly offered by a restaurant in China.

Toilet humour is another favourite. 'Fresh soft stools on display' has been spotted by several readers outside a furniture shop in the USA, while 'do not drop butts' is a common sign found next to Asian lavatories. Visitors might not thank the sign that forbids 'personal hygiene in this area', while that which warns people not to drink the urinal water might be a little too obvious for most.

The casual, often disastrous

misnaming of services is another rich source of amusement. Take Moron Constructions, for example, a company that brilliantly fails to inspire confidence in its craftsmanship, or Salon Ridiculous where visitors might expect to leave with a hilarious hairstyle.

Then there are the unfortunate coincidences, such as the Spanish town of Poo, or the inexplicable phrases, like the Chinese tourist site which 'Heartly welcome you in open defecation'. Or even the plain unwise, such as the Panicker's tourist bus service in Delhi.

So let us thank those kind-hearted shop and hotel owners, and their trusting dependence on unreliable internet translation tools, and be glad that we have them to enliven our travels. Let us be grateful, then, and raise a glass – perhaps of 'Poo Water', or, indeed, 'Arse' wine.

ROAD SIGNS

Are we nearly there yet?

While car journeys can sometimes be long and boring, they can also be hilarious, as this chapter shows. *Sign Language* invites you to join in a rib-tickling game of I Spy as we present some of the most amusing signs spotted from car windows all over the world.

Imagine plotting a road trip to Poo in Spain, via a host of other ludicrous place names. After handing around the car-sickness tablets in Pukeberg, Sweden, a fitting end to the journey might be a drive to Witts End in south Wales.

But confusing signs can also be a major source of irritation for motorists. Knowing your right from your left is a basic childhood skill and one that should be essential for anyone installing road signs. And yet often we are left scratching our heads as contradictory signposts ask us to turn right above arrows that point left, or suggest two opposing directions for the same destination.

Roadworks can also make a motorist's blood boil. But for English-speaking drivers in Denmark they become a journey highlight, thanks to the liberal use of the word 'fart'. The signs found here are actually advising motorists to lessen their speed but should be applauded for creating the world's only traffic jams where people queue with smiles on their faces.

INDECISIVENESS AWAITS →
Location: 2.25 miles from Llantwit Major, Wales
Spotted by: Steph Jones

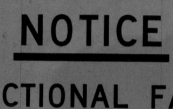

NOTICE

CORRECTIONAL FACILITY
DO NOT STOP
FOR HITCHHIKERS

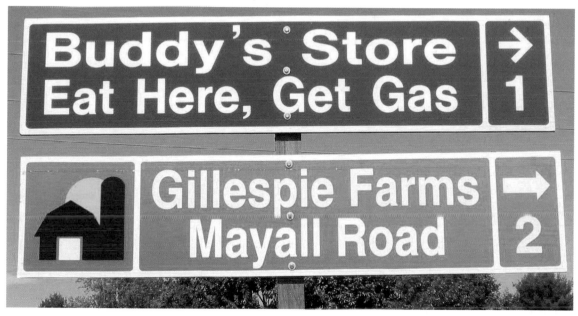

← **GIVEN THE SLIPROAD**
Location: Colorado, USA
Spotted by: Simon Meek

↑ **GAS 'N' GULP**
Location: Maine, USA
Spotted by: Sandra Dudley

↑ **CARP ARK**
Location: Colorado, USA
Spotted by: Beth Cuilla

← **ONE HUMP OR TWO?**
Location: Dubai
Spotted by: Craig and Gill

→ **ALL ROADS LEAD TO SPAIN**
Location: Gibraltar
Spotted by: Barbara Wicker

→ **YOU'RE FIRED**
Location: Virginia, USA
Spotted by: John Pratt

→ **THE END OF THE ROAD**
Location: Colorado, USA
Spotted by: Mike Johnson

← **CAR SICK**
Location: Sweden
Spotted by: Dave Sturtz

↑ **NO TURNING BACK**
Location: Rhondda, Wales
Spotted by: Algwyn Myring

← **CONFUSION REIGNS**
Location: Melbourne, Australia
Spotted by: George Topfner

→ **JUST PASSING THROUGH**
Location: Asturias, Northern Spain
Spotted by: Graham Renshaw

→ **SENSE OF DIRECTION**
Location: Chester, UK
Spotted by: Keith Hughes

→ **ME-OWWWW!**
Location: unknown
Spotted by: Phil Chivers

← **SPEED KILLS**
Location: Teesdale, UK
Spotted by: Nick Hume

↑ **EMOTIONAL CUL-DE-SAC**
Location: Brynsadler, South Wales
Spotted by: Deborah St John

← **HOLY SMOKE**
Location: Kilcoy, Australia
Spotted by: Joe Bisco

→ **HEAD FIRST**
Location: Venice, Italy
Spotted by: Simon James

→ RIDICULOUSLY
PUBLIC TPYO
Location: unknown
Spotted by: Eric Penner

→ IIOLD IT IN
Location: Denmark
Spotted by: Tim Carnell

← ZERO INTOLERANCE
Location: Cape Town, South Africa
Spotted by: Frances Phillips

↑ **IN SAFE HANDS**
Location: Delhi, India
Spotted by: Lynda Young

← **BEWARE! PSYCHOTIC TRUCKERS**
Location: Hainan, China
Spotted by: Paul Tibbenham

→ **FLIPPIN' 'ECK**
Location: Lochty, Scotland
Spotted by: Philip Hannah

→ **RIDDLE ROAD**
Location: Tynemouth, UK
Spotted by: Graham Jacob

→ **MARKED CAR**
Location: Dorset, UK
Spotted by: Derek Washington

← **TOP GRRRR**
Location: Taif, Saudi Arabia
Spotted by: Chris Deveney

FOOD AND DRINK

It's a staple of any trip away; menu-gazing, and tittering at mistranslations and bloopers, can become a mealtime ritual.

The internet has given tourists a whole new helping, as you will see here. To a busy restaurateur, it might have seemed a godsend. Now you can provide alluring descriptions of dishes in any language: simply stick your menu through an online translation programme, and a culinary Tower of Babel can be yours.

Except it doesn't always work. As 'Lubina to the garlic pescador' shows, such menus have the power to bamboozle; they can also startle ('explodes the large intestine'); and, at their most unfortunate, they may put you off your meal altogether.

Misplaced consonants are a more traditional howler – also well represented in these pages – and can have equally devastating consequences. This is when fried 'carp' becomes something altogether less appealing; worse perhaps than 'sweat corn'.

Food and drink brand names, meanwhile – so important to pitch right – can be fraught with danger if unchecked with an international crowd. Fancy some refreshing, iced 'Poo Water'? Or how about a glass of vintage 'Arse' wine?

But the final word – as is traditional for cuisine – should go to the French. Thanks to the vagaries of online translation, a sophisticated restaurant advertised one of its specials as 'grilled paving stone'. Beat that, Heston Blumenthal.

WARNING SIGN →
Location: Hong Kong
Spotted by: Richard Cameron

皇海鮮酒家
NASTY Seafood Restaurant

米 北角站 North Point Station

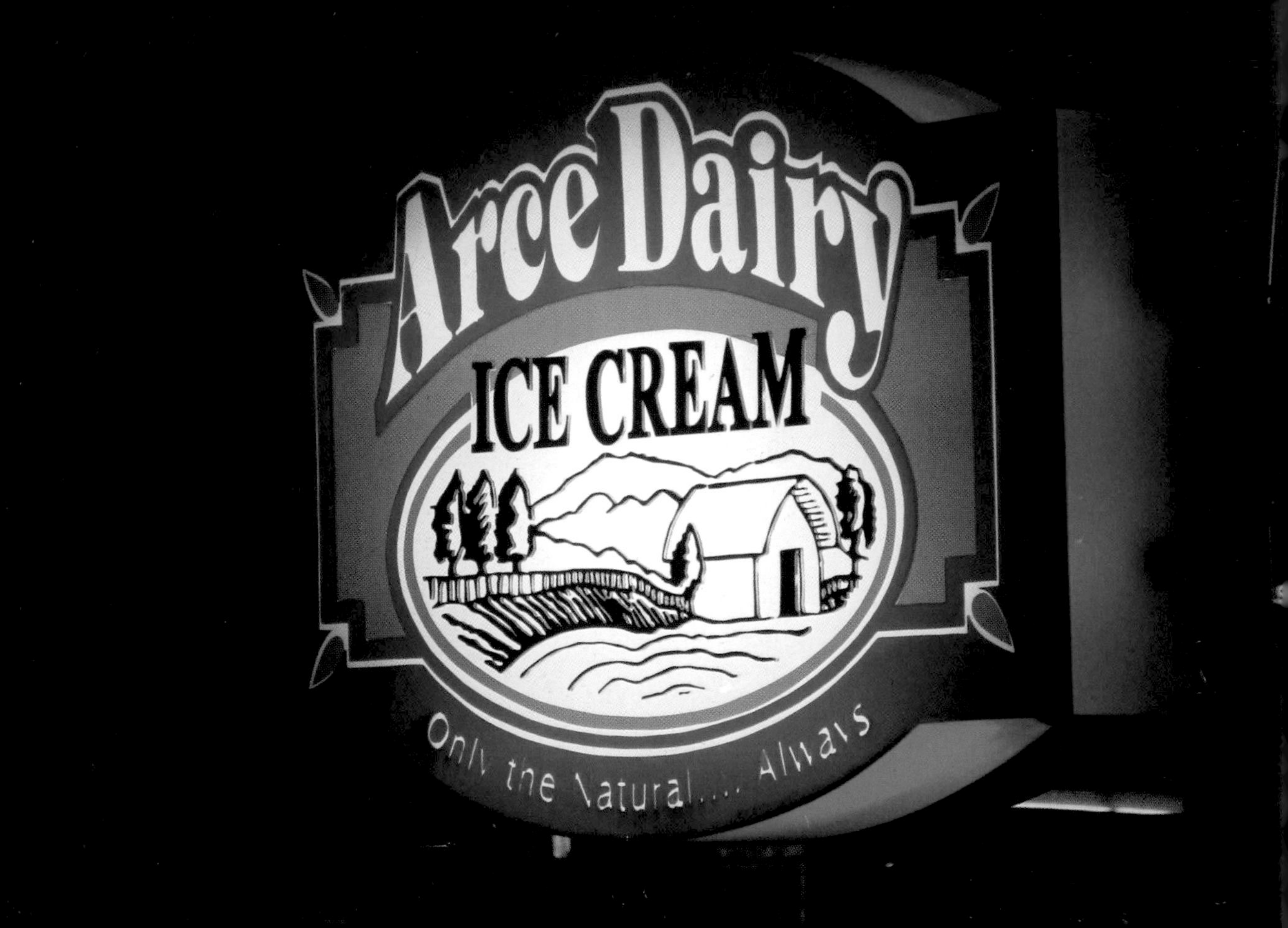
Arce Dairy
ICE CREAM
Only the Natural.... Always

← **MY STOMACH IS CHURNING**
Location: Manila, Philippines
Spotted by: Doug Munro

→ **THE MORNING AFTER**
Location: Lyon, France
Spotted by: Patrick Daly

↑ **WAITER, THERE'S A FROG IN MY PORRIDGE**
Location: Singapore
Spotted by: Stuart Adams

← **PLACED BETWEEN TWO BUNS**
Location: Baltimore, USA
Spotted by: Bill Murphy

→ **OR EATEE INEE?**
Location: Nova Scotia, Canada
Spotted by: Lisa Davis-Walker

HOU'S TAKEE OUTEE

頂 **893-0011** 好

FREE DELIVERY

KILANG PENGELUARAN MAKANAN
SOON FATT FOOD COMPANY

→ TASTY
Location: Callao, Peru
Spotted by: Robin Somes

→ HAM FISTED
Location: Maine, USA
Spotted by: Mark Bigelow

← ALL YOU CAN EAT
Location: Kuala Lumpur, Malaysia
Spotted by: Don Miller

↑ **COLD SEAT**
Location: tub of ice cream,
Bosnia and Herzegovina
Spotted by: Stephen Croft

← **THE HANNIBAL SPECIAL**
Location: Chinese restaurant, Twickenham, UK
Spotted by: Keith Treble

→ **FULL OF BEANS**
Location: Khmelnitsky, Ukraine
Spotted by: Rachel Graham

桃の滴　大吟醸（伏見　松本酒造）
Momonoshizuku - Daiginjo

¥ 3694

呑口に広がる香りは、フルーティーな桃の香りがする吟醸香と、
かすかな餅の香りを感じることができる豊かな香りを持つ素晴らしい吟醸酒です。

Bung hole spread aroma is fragrant with the aroma of peach fruity sake,
Ginjo sake has a wonderful rich flavor you can feel a faint aroma of rice.

← 'CLEAN-UP ON
AISLE SEVEN!'
Location: Romania
Spotted by: Leigh Virkus

↑ PEACHY BUNG HOLE
Location: Kyoto, Japan
Spotted by: Ben Janssens

↑ **CORKED**
Location: unknown
Spotted by: Robin Stokes

← **MIXED BAG**
Location: Singapore
Spotted by: Ted Higgs

→ **SERVED BY THE SLAB**
Location: Paris, France
Spotted by: Ian Rees

Raclette au Jambon cru.................16
(400g de fromage / cheese 400g)
Raclette au Grison.......................18
(400g de fromage / cheese 400g)
Pavé Grillé.................................14
Grilled paving stone
Pavé au Poivre...........................16
Paving stone with pepper sauce
Tartiflette et sa salade verte..........14
Tartiflette and green salad
Boeuf Bourguignon......................12
Filet Mignon de Porc....................12

早餐肠

Intestinal Breakfast

← MORNING GORY
Location: China
Spotted by: Ian Moulson

→ ONE RUMP OR TWO?
Location: Paris, France
Spotted by: Hal Stinchfield

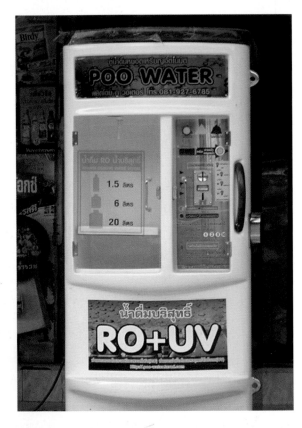

FISHES

HAKE TO THE OVEN WITH CLAMS	17 €
NAPE OF HAKE TO THE OVEN WITH SHRIMPS	17 €
GOLDEN OF THE SMALLEST SEA TO SAL	15 €
LUBINA TO THE GARLIC PESCADOR	15 €
ROOSTER FRIED PEDRO WITH TENDER GARLICS, CENSUS PEPPERS AND POTATOES TO THE POOR THING	20 €
AMERICAN LOBSTER WITH MUSSELS, PRAWNS AND PELLETS OF POTATO	15 €

↑ **POOR PEDRO**
Location: San Pedro del Pinatar, Alicante, Spain
Spotted by: Peter Clarke

← **DON'T DRINK THE WATER**
Location: Saraburi, Thailand
Spotted by: Michael W Waller

→ **FOOD FOR THOUGHT**
Location: Dubai
Spotted by: Peter Hobbs

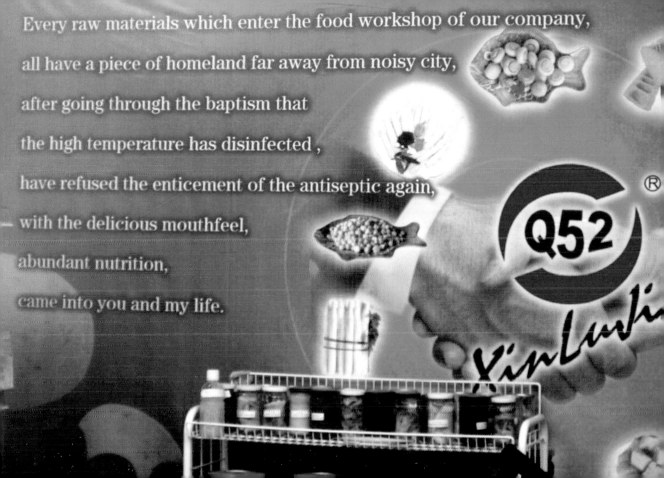

Every raw materials which enter the food workshop of our company,

all have a piece of homeland far away from noisy city,

after going through the baptism that

the high temperature has disinfected ,

have refused the enticement of the antiseptic again,

with the delicious mouthfeel,

abundant nutrition,

came into you and my life.

Q52 ®

XinLuli

Chocolate Mousse
Cream Pie
House Special
Buganvilia Sweet
Biscuit Cake
Camel Dribal
Fruit Salad
Strawberries w/ Cream (on
Pie W/ Ice Cream

repes/ Crepe

← HOT AND COLD
Location: Tibet
Spotted by: Adem Normaal

↑ DROOLING OVER THE MENU
Location: Portugal
Spotted by: Alfie

Food menu

北京老方

Dumpling 水饺	¥25
ShanChaGao 山楂糕	¥20
Hand-rolling bread 手卷饼	¥10
modification 凉粉	¥20
Meatballs powder 肉丸粉面	¥25
Yangzhou rice 扬州炒饭	¥20
Beijing jajangmyun 北京炸酱面	¥25
Single cake box 单饼盒子	¥10
The cold noodles 凉拌面	¥20
Meat buns 肉夹馍	¥10
The cold noodles 凉拌面	¥20
Fried noodles 炒刀削面	¥28
Stir-fry noodle 炒拉面	¥28
Mix liangpi 拌凉皮	¥20
Sichuan-style modification 川味凉粉	¥20
Hand noodle 手拉面	¥25
noodles 刀削面	¥25
Flavor 风味米线	¥25
Fleshy foam 肉沫米线	¥25
Casserole dish 砂锅米线	¥28
Beijing Fried rice 北京炒饭	¥28
Stir-fry powder 炒粉	¥25
Fried 炒面	¥25

Sour and popping rice — noodles
Sichuan style (酸辣粉).

Modification

Beijing jajangmyun

Yangzhou rice

Single cake box

Meat buns

KITCHEN ASSISTENT REQUIRED,

GOOD ENGLISH ESSENCIAL, APPLY WITHIN

↑ **BARE ESSENCIALS**
Location: Leicester Square, London, UK
Spotted by: Kieran Meeke

← **MENU MADNESS**
Location: Shenzhen, China
Spotted by: Ian M Dickinson

→ **WITH CRISPY WHISKERS**
Location: Sepang, Malaysia
Spotted by: Mike Doodson

KUQRAT CAFÉ ®

REG: (001607341-T)
MPSPG 6/BBST/05/2006

DIMILIKI OLE

KUQRAT CAFE

TRANSIT ROOM & TRANSPORT SERVICE KLIA
03-8706 /016- &017-236 8961
24 HOUR

10

KUQRAT
CAFE
KOPIT I. H

flavoured with ...

◆ **Reshmi Kabab**
Boneless Julliene of chicken Marinated in white spices and curd

◆ **Kakori Kabab**
Finely Minced Lamb Blended with mild spices with black pep
being mor predominant

◆ **Galouti Kabab**
Fine velvet smooth mice kabab flavoured with cardamom

Note: We Levy 10% Servic

→ WHAT'S EATING
GILBERT'S GRAPES?
Location: Denmark
Spotted by: Jonathan Lowth

← SQUEAK AND SOUR
Location: Hotel Godwin,
Delhi, India
Spotted by: Heidi Campbell

In Great Britain, it's estimated that 92,749 liters of beer each year are lost in beer drinker special hair

↑ **ABSOLUTELY DRIPPING**
Location: Hyderabad, India
Spotted by: Clifford Bowles

← **AND THAT'S A FACT!**
Location: Ho Chi Minh City, Vietnam
Spotted by: Nick Marchorst

→ **FIT FOR A KING**
Location: Kagoshima, Japan
Spotted by: Keith Berry

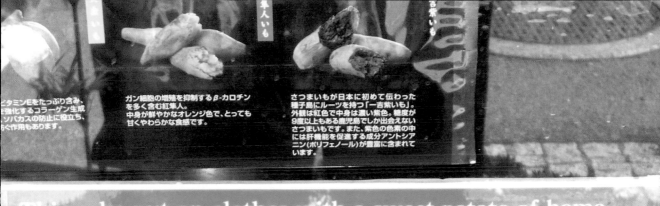

ビタミンEをたっぷり含み、
化するコラーゲン生成
、ソバカスの防止に役立ち、
ぐ作用もあります。

ガン細胞の増殖を抑制するβ-カロチン
を多く含む紅隼人。
中身が鮮やかなオレンジ色で、とっても
甘くやわらかな食感です。

さつまいもが日本に初めて伝わった
種子島にルーツを持つ「一吉紫いも」。
外観は紅色で中身は濃い紫色。糖度が
9度以上もある鹿児島でしか出会えない
さつまいもです。また、紫色の色素の中
には肝機能を促進する成分アントシア
ニン(ポリフェノール)が豊富に含まれて
います。

This cake put on clothes with a sweet potato of home
Kagoshima as bean jam around and baked it.
It is a very healthy cake of high quality which His Majesty
the Emperor ate.
Please enjoy sampling by all means in a shop.
I have you buy even one.

DUNG

RESTAURANT VIETNAMIEN

AL'B

← HMM, TEMPTING...
Location: Paris, France
Spotted by: David Dixit

↑ GUARANTEED TO
GET YOU ON YOUR FEET
Location: Suriname
Spotted by: Barclay Miller

↑ HARD TO STOMACH
Location: Tokyo, Japan
Spotted by: Mark Everett

↑ BEWARE THE AFTER-EFFECTS
Location: Bangkok, Thailand
Spotted by: David Parry

$52(例)
標記酥炸大腸
Explodes the large intestine

↑ THUNDERPANTS
Location: Hong Kong
Spotted by: Ian Clarke

→ CEREAL KILLER
Location: Singapore
Spotted by: Sue McNicol

MAFIA PORRIDGE

52

LEASING ENQUIRIES

A hotel sign in Pattaya, Thailand, advertises its amenities: 'Porn. Laundry. Room for rent.' Is this useful prioritisation or the (unfortunate) name of the proprietor? We'll never know, but when hotels provide signs and translated notices for their guests, they so often get it wrong.

Consider the tired traveller seeking some much-needed pampering in a Hong Kong hotel, and finding a 'Do not scream' sign displayed in their massage therapy room. Or the guest at Gold Grand China Hotel in Guangzhou, wondering why he might need to order a 'gas mask' or 'hand grenade' from the hotel amenities menu, listed alongside the extra pillowcases.

Then there are the hotel names, such as 'Hotel Bimbo' in Skopje, Macedonia, an establishment which doesn't appear to hold its clientele in very high esteem.

You might be nervous about ordering a drink at the Hilton in Sharm-el-Sheikh, where a sign politely informs guests that they 'Apologise for incontinences'. A particular Scottish establishment, meanwhile, instructs its guests that 'On no account must hot bottoms be placed on the worktops'.

Even that, though, is perhaps preferable to eating at the Riviera Maya restaurant in Mexico, where a table is conspicuously reserved for 'Mr Death'.

HOTELS

ELEVATOR MUSIC →
Location: lift in Copenhagen
Spotted by: Dave Sturtz

Dear guests,

Kindly be informed that Chill out Bar will be
closed today from 18:00 till 19:00.
We do apologize for incontinences.
Thank you for understanding,

Hotel Management

Уважаемые гости,
Мы хотели бы Вас проинформировать,
что Chill out Bar не будет работать сегодня
с 18:00 до 19:00.
Мы извиняемся за возникшие неудобства

↑ DIRTY WASHING
Location: Pattaya, Thailand
Spotted by: Nick Pearsons

→ THE LAST SUPPER
Location: Riviera Maya restaurant, Mexico
Spotted by: Charlie Aikman

← HOLD IT IN
Location: Hilton, Sharm-el-Sheikh, Egypt
Spotted by: Nicole Cummins

MEMONTOS FOR GUESTS

1. Wish you that do not smoke in ger caused on provide safety of conflagration.
2. Do not dump chaffs, make open fire and defecate near the complex. Please only dump into dedicated pin.
3. Admonish to access pets in ger.
4. Admonish hardly, to cook meals on appliances and to plug electric heating in ger.
5. Do not forget to lock the door when you leave from ger.
6. Please receive to see types of service and price list at our complex from manager at reception service.
7. It will keep for 2 /two/ months if you forget your ownership.
8. In other times of service in ger, do not use to carry out cups, dishes, spoons, forks and other things in restaurant to ger.
9. Do not carry out the inventories in ger.
10. Admonish hardly, to bring to use intoxicant drinks in bar and restaurant from out.
11. Wish you do not rattle and break rest time and comport of other guests and behaving respectfully.
12. If you flee and break any things in ger, you will pay registered price of them.
13. Wish that you pay the fees in terms when you stayed in ger before 12AM of afterdate and please give back inventories in ger to waitress.

"SHONKHOR GOVI" Co.,ltd

← **GER CRAZY**
Location: Gobi Tours Ger Camp, Mongolia
Spotted by: Jay Selley

→ **PERFECT FOR LONG STAYS**
Location: France
Spotted by: John Varnham

HOTEL - MOURGUE

FROMAGERIE

...CIALITES

FROMAGERIE

SPIRITUEUX

HOTEL

Bimbo

↑ MASSAAAAAAAARGE!

Location: massage therapy room in Hong Kong
Spotted by: Shahnaz Guivi

→ THOSE THINGS COST A BOMB

Location: Gold Grand China Hotel, Guangzhou, China
Spotted by: Navjot Singh

← BEST FOR BLONDES

Location: Skopje, Macedonia
Spotted by: Ron Manle

请勿喧哗

DO NOT SCREAM

...ods for you in the room. If you have an inte...
...act the House keeping dept(dial "6").
...ur hotel wish you have good trip!

价格	物品	价格
¥350.00	茶叶盂 Tea Handleless Cup	
¥280.00	玻璃烟灰碟（套） Ashtray(class)	¥10.00
¥250.00	陶瓷烟灰碟 Ashtray(chinaware)	¥25.00
¥230.00	皂碟 Soap dish	¥5.00
¥180.00	咖啡杯带碟 Coffee cup and dish	¥5.00
¥150.00	文件夹 Folder	¥35.00
¥120.00	便签垫 Memo pad	¥150.00
¥100.00	拖线板 Adapter	¥50.00
¥80.00	广州市工商黄页 Telephone Book	¥70.00
¥60.00	电吹风筒 Hair dryer	¥250.00
¥50.00	网线 Broad Band Wire	¥180.00
¥40.00	防毒面具 Gas Mask	¥30.00
¥70.00	灭火桶 Hand Grenade	¥250.00
¥30.00	防滑垫 Bath mat	¥250.00
¥15.00		¥50.00
¥60.00		
¥350.00		
¥35.00		
¥25.00		
¥20.00		
¥40.00		
¥800.00		
¥250.00		
¥150.00		

NOTICE TO STAFF

Will ladies please
rinse out teapots,
then stand upside down in sink

ON NO ACCOUNT

Must hot bottoms be
placed on the worktops.

NOTICE

HAND BASINS

Dear Members,

Please be kind enough to adhere to the following rules:

1. DO NOT wash your clothes or underwear in the HAND Basin.
2. DO NOT wash yourself in the HAND Basin, Please use the showers that have been provided.
3. DO NOT shave your privates over the HAND Basin
4. Please drain your dirty water out after use
5. Please use a Towel to cover yourself not a face cloth

Please consider your fellow members.

↑ **NO HEADSTANDS OR PROLONGED SITTING**
Location: Scotland
Spotted by: Cathy Reckenberg

↑ **CLOSE SHAVE**
Location: Johannesburg, South Africa
Spotted by: J Wismark

→ **BOX OF DELIGHTS**
Location: Yunnan, China
Spotted by: Mike Vose

温馨提示
Warm prompt

欢迎您入住迪庆观光酒店.盒
welcome to sightseeing hotel

内一次性用品请无偿使用。
please volunteer use the disposable thing in box.

此盒为非赠品。
This box is not prescnt.

谢 谢
Thank you

TOILET HUMOUR

There's something decidedly unnerving about the prospect of a foreign lavatory. Anyone familiar with the smallest room in your average Thai hostel – or Glaswegian pub, for that matter – will no doubt agree.

We've become accustomed to spotless ceramics and double-quilted paper at home. Head abroad, though, and there's a good chance you'll find yourself gingerly placing your used toilet paper into a miniature dustbin and – in the case of many South-East Asian hostels – washing away the wickedness with a filth-encrusted bucket. And who can forget the first time they encountered a 'squatter' – a lavatory that is little more than a hole in the ground?

Overseas latrines throw up enough defecatory dilemmas without the prospect of stumbling across a sign declaring that 'personal hygiene is forbidden', you must 'flash after use', and under no circumstances are you to 'press knob with force'.

But toilet humour need not end in the bathroom. There's the picturesque French village of Arses, a chain of restaurants in Spain called Ars, and the wonderfully-named L'il Stool House of Ottawa. Why do we find humour in such puerile pastures? And is there a single English-speaking man who hasn't contemplated removing the 'L' from the 'SWIMMING POOL' sign at his local leisure centre? We think not.

A CRACKING PLACE TO LIVE →
Location: Aveyron, France
Spotted by: Lou Maitland-Hudson

... of equal or lessor price FREE

All Cow & Horse Poo Paper
now 25% off

El hotel no se hace responsable por valores

We are not responsible for lost or

Prohibido realizarse higiene personal en este lugar

Personal hygiene in this area is forbidden

← **ROLL UP**
Location: South Australia
Spotted by: Joy Stokes

↑ **IT WON'T WASH**
Location: Quito, Ecuador
Spotted by: Dave Amos

↑ **BOTTOM FEEDER**
Location: Madrid, Spain
Spotted by: Kevin Day

↑ **WHAT A DUMP**
Location: Ottawa, Canada
Spotted by: Jim Garner

→ **ONE AT A TIME, PLEASE**
Location: Yellowstone National
Park, USA
Spotted by: Della Murton

"सरसफाइ आफुले मात्र गरेर पुर्दैन
अरुलाई पनि सिकाउनुहोस"

"खुला दिसा मुक्त गा. वि. स. बन्दिपुर
मा यहाँलाई हार्दिक स्वागत छ।

HEARTLY WELCOME TO YOU IN OPEN
DEFECATION FREE V.D.C. BANDIPUR

बन्दिपुर गा. वि. स.

↑ **SPECIAL DELIVERY**
Location: Shanghai, China
Spotted by: Thomas Egeter

→ **TICKET TOOT**
Location: Locarno, Switzerland
Spotted by: 'ER'

← **NO MESSING AROUND**
Location: Bandipur, Nepal
Spotted by: Winkie Pickthall

↑ THAT SHRINKING FEELING
Location: Vienna, Austria
Spotted by: Scott Montgomery

↑ UP TO YOUR NECK IN IT
Location: Kent, UK
Spotted by: Tim Alden

→ LOO GOT TO BE JOKING
Location: Chengdu, China
Spotted by: Thomas Wilson

男性卫生间
The male sex toilet

PASSA A WIND
E RADDOPPI LE RICARICHE!

↑ **BLOWN AWAY**
Location: Cairns, Australia
Spotted by: Andrea Lane

→ **PEE WARNED!**
Location: Phuket, Thailand
Spotted by: Paul Lattimore

← **WHAT A GAS**
Location: Italy
Spotted by: Mal Parr

← **A MUST-PEE EXHIBITION**
Location: Machynlleth, Wales
Spotted by: John Waddington

← **INDECENT DISPOSAL**
Location: Beijing, China
Spotted by: Grainne Loughran

→ **HIT AND HOPE**
Location: Florida, USA
Spotted by: Peter Hoyles

THIS FACILITY IS HANDS FREE

MEN →

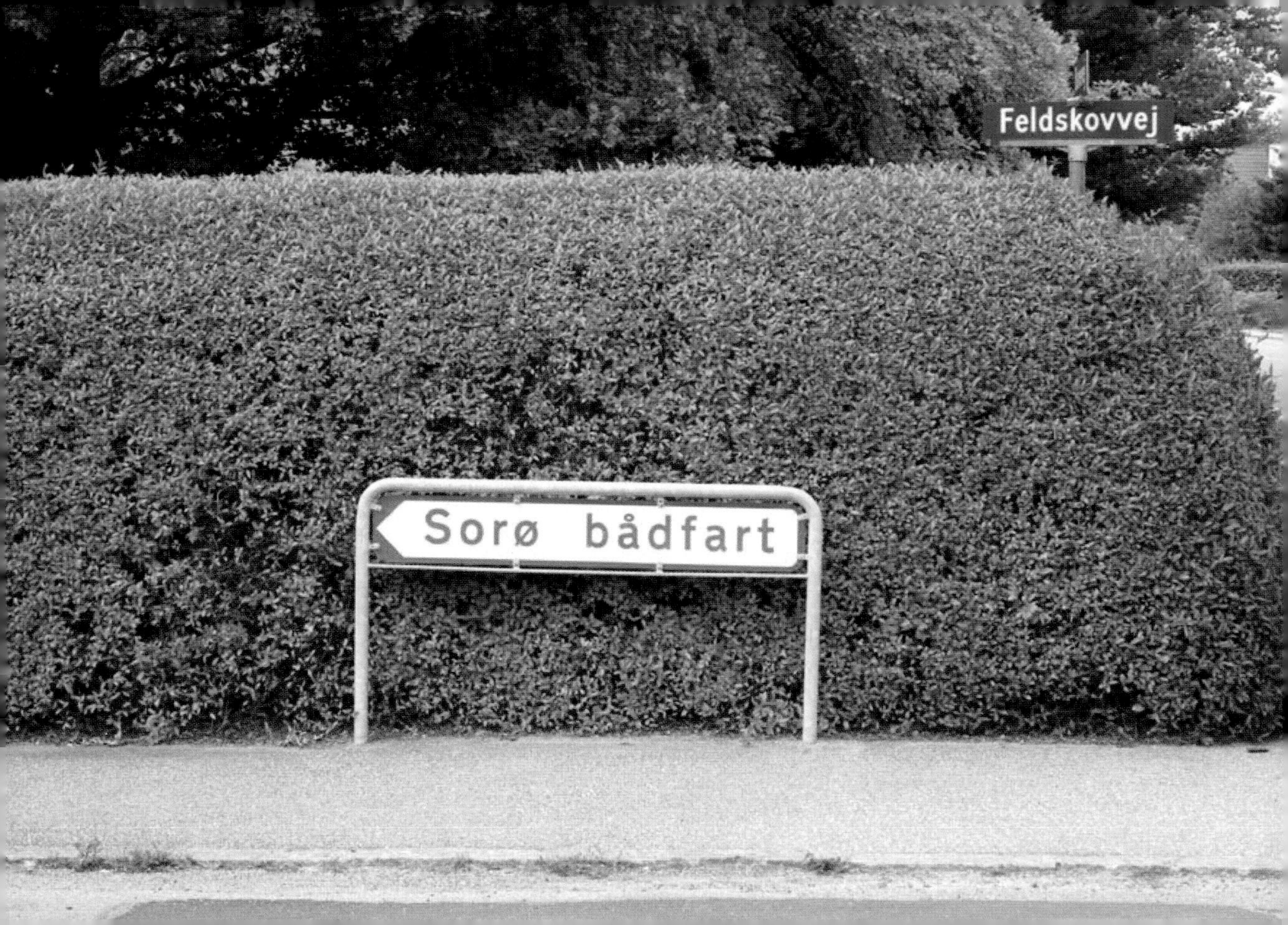
Feldskovvej
Sorø bådfart

↑ FRENCH FOR GAS
Location: Quebec City, Canada
Spotted by: Chris and Karen Evans

→ HANDLE WITH CARE
Location: Accra, Ghana
Spotted by: Jonathan Wells

← WINDY CITY
Location: Sorø, Denmark
Spotted by: Phil Smart

↑ DON'T FENCE ME IN
Location: unknown
Spotted by: Michael Rolfe

↑ SOUND ADVICE
Location: Taichung, Taiwan
Spotted by: Tom Odlin

→ BOWL OF FOOD
Location: Turkey
Spotted by: Will Flewett

1. Bitte kein Toilettenpapier ins WC werfen, sondern in den danebenstehenden Eimer, er wird täglich während dem Frühstück von der Mannschaft geleert.

2. Nach getaner Arbeit wird gespült, stellen Sie den <u>kleinen Hebel nach links</u> und pumpen Sie Wasser Schüssel.

3. Nachher stellen Sie den <u>Hebel nach rechts</u> und pumpen, bis die Schüssel leer ist, plus zusätzlich noc ca. 10x.

Please do not put anything into the toilet, until You have eaten it first.

1. Please don't through toiletpaper into the toilet, all kind of rubbish need to go into the small basket cl the toilet. Basket will be daily cleaned by crew member during breakfast.

2. After your toilet job is done you must turn the small handle left direction and pump water into the tol

3. Little bit after please turn handle right direction and pump please till toilet is completly empty bi and at least please 10 times more pumping.

Does the creator of Throttleman boxer shorts realise his business faces daily ridicule? Are the good folk at Moron Constructions blissfully unaware that English-speaking customers will never take them seriously?

Shopping excursions provide a sizeable proportion of our readers' photographic submissions. But are our unlucky shopkeepers aware that the steady stream of camera-wielding tourists are pointing and laughing because their shop has a silly name? Or do the giggling handful of foreigners simply foster a growing sense of paranoia among those innocent retailers?

Several eagle-eyed travellers have spotted Semen Market in Istanbul, while a purveyor of timepieces in Izmir, who had the wherewithal to add the sign 'Genuine Fake Watches' next to his stall, has been photographed by at least a dozen *Telegraph* readers.

Perhaps they are aware of their shops' mirthful names. Is it simply a cunning ploy to attract visitors, drum up business and watch the tourist dollars roll in? Come for the photo, stay for the fake Rolex? Perhaps, although that does little to explain the choice of branding for the Ass Hair Salon in Beijing.

SHOPPING

THE REAL DEAL →
Location: Izmir, Turkey
Spotted by: Matthew R Goulding

PASHMINA SILK SUNGLASSES HAT
CASHMERE SHAWL BATTERIES BOOKS

TAKSİ

GENUINE FAKE WATCHES

35 T 6080

Shoe Zone

BUY 1 GET 1 FREE

FREE

BUY 1 GET 1 FREE

FREE

BUY 1 FREE

9.99   4.9   4.99   14.99

BUY 1 GET 1 FREE

FREE 6.99

BUY 1 GET 1 FREE

BUY 1 GET 1 FR E

BUY 1 GET 1 FR E

↑ **CAN'T FIND WHAT YOU'RE LOOKING FOR?**
Location: Hong Kong
Spotted by: Uwe

→ **CRACKING THE MARKET**
Location: Beijing, China
Spotted by: Mark Sullivan

← **SHOES WISELY**
Location: Guildford, UK
Spotted by: Melvyn Hayward

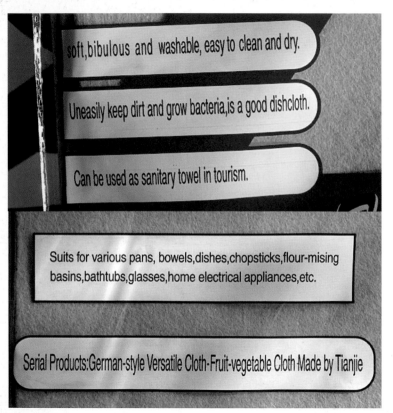

soft,bibulous and washable, easy to clean and dry.

Uneasily keep dirt and grow bacteria,is a good dishcloth.

Can be used as sanitary towel in tourism.

Suits for various pans, bowels,dishes,chopsticks,flour-mising basins,bathtubs,glasses,home electrical appliances,etc.

Serial Products:German-style Versatile Cloth-Fruit-vegetable Cloth-Made by Tianjie

← **WONDERCLOTH**
Location: Dhaka, Bangladesh
Spotted by: Andrew Lovedee-Turner

→ **COME IN PEACE**
Location: Beijing, China
Spotted by: Steve Alexander

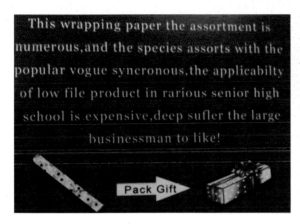

This wrapping paper the assortment is numerous, and the species assorts with the popular vogue syncronous, the applicabilty of low file product in rarious senior high school is expensive, deep sufler the large businessman to like!

Pack Gift

↑ **THAT'S A WRAP**
Location: London, UK
Spotted by: Sophie Ainscough

→ **THIS PLACE IS ALWAYS HEAVING**
Location: Bangkok, Thailand
Spotted by: Thomas Wilson

← **A TRUSTED BRAND**
Location: Jesolo, Italy
Spotted by: Bob Boycott

タイ本場のマッサージ

miss

Puke

THAI TRADITION MASSAGE
● FOOT MASSAGE
● THAI MASSAGE
● OIL MASSAGE
● AROMATHERAPY

TEL. 02-251-6591

WWW.misspuke.net

← **PLEASE, CALL ME RICHARD**
Location: New South Wales, Australia
Spotted by: Joelle Khalife

→ **THICK AS A BRICK**
Location: Dordogne, France
Spotted by: Sarah Fletcher

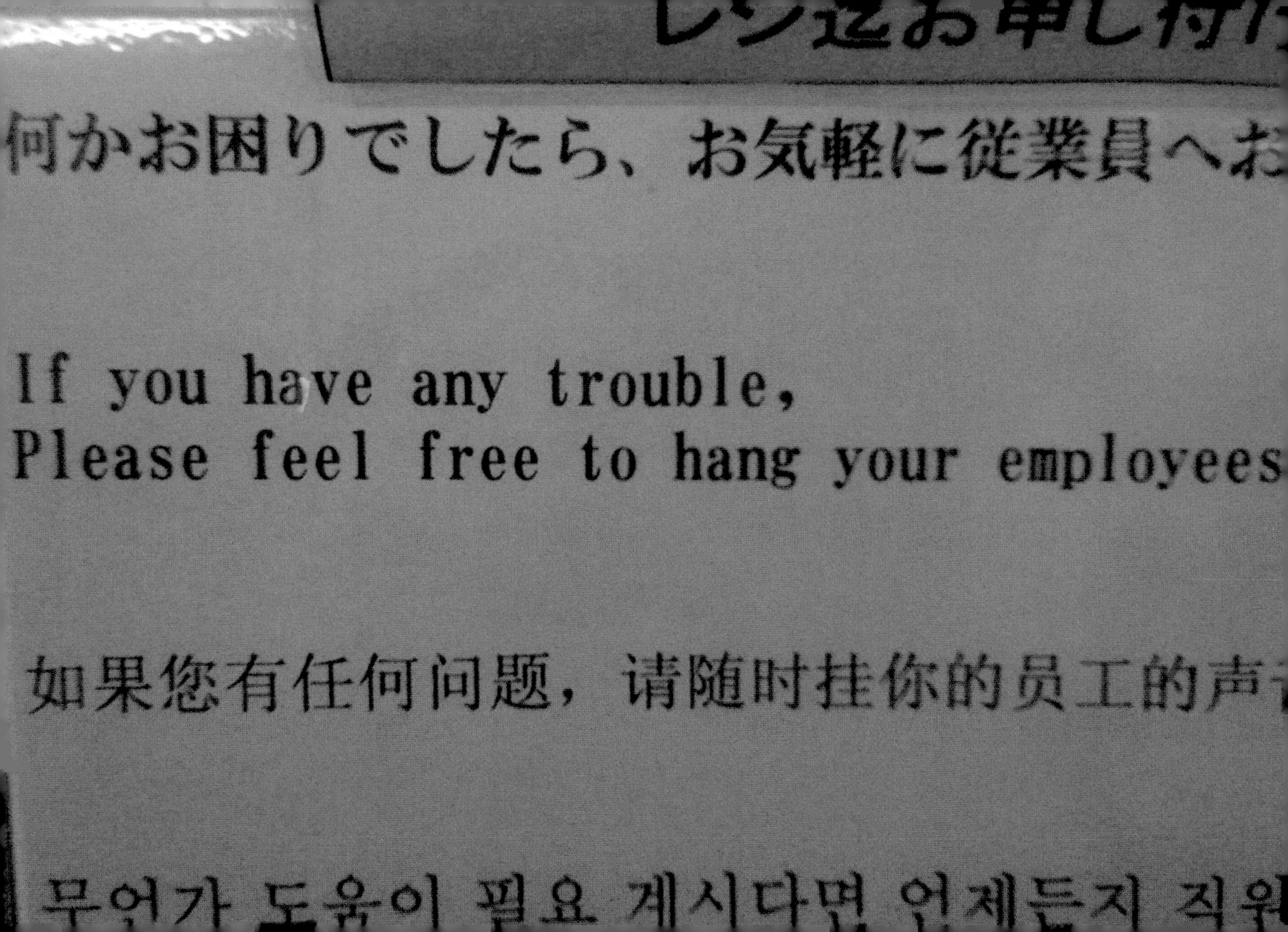

何かお困りでしたら、お気軽に従業員へお

If you have any trouble,
Please feel free to hang your employees

如果您有任何问题，请随时挂你的员工的声

무엇가 도움이 필요 계시다면 언제든지 직원

→ **DON'T MOVE A MUSCLE**
Location: Beijing, China
Spotted by: Emma Rae

← **SWING BY THE OFFICE**
Location: Japan
Spotted by: Robin Probyn

↑ **WELL SPOTTED**
Location: unknown
Spotted by: David Cox

→ **FANGS FOR THE FILLING**
Location: Bangalore, India
Spotted by: Pradeep Lal

↑ **TIGHT FITTING**
Location: Albufeira, Portugal
Spotted by: Colin Barson

→ **THEY MUST BE NUTS!**
Location: supermarket, Al Ain, UAE
Spotted by: Paul Beltrami

← **BUREAU DE CHIMP**
Location: Bali
Spotted by: Muzzy and Anna

↑ **YOU LOOK HILARIOUS!**
Location: Sri Lanka
Spotted by: Savitrit

← **ENGLAND ÜBER ALLES**
Location: Beijing, China
Spotted by: Jonathan Watkins

→ **THIS MAY HURT A BIT**
Location: Washington, USA
Spotted by: C Simon Farrow

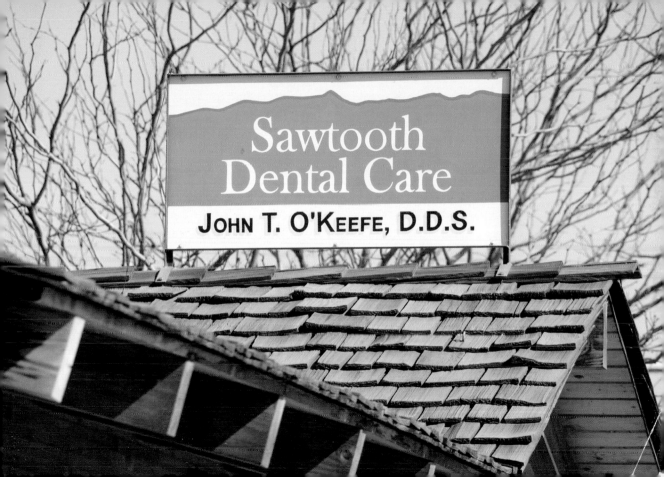

→ **ART NO NO**
Location: Sylt, Germany
Spotted by: Stefan Horn

← **SURELY 'SPERM BANK'?**
Location: Istanbul, Turkey
Spotted by: Kyle Helkc

← **CROOKED SMILE**
Location: Kawakawa, Bay of Islands, New Zealand
Spotted by: Ken Donelan

← **STEP INTO MY THING PLACE**
Location: Hanzhong, China
Spotted by: Ron Sanders

→ **HAIR TODAY, GONE TOMORROW**
Location: Taiwan
Spotted by: Lawrence Walker

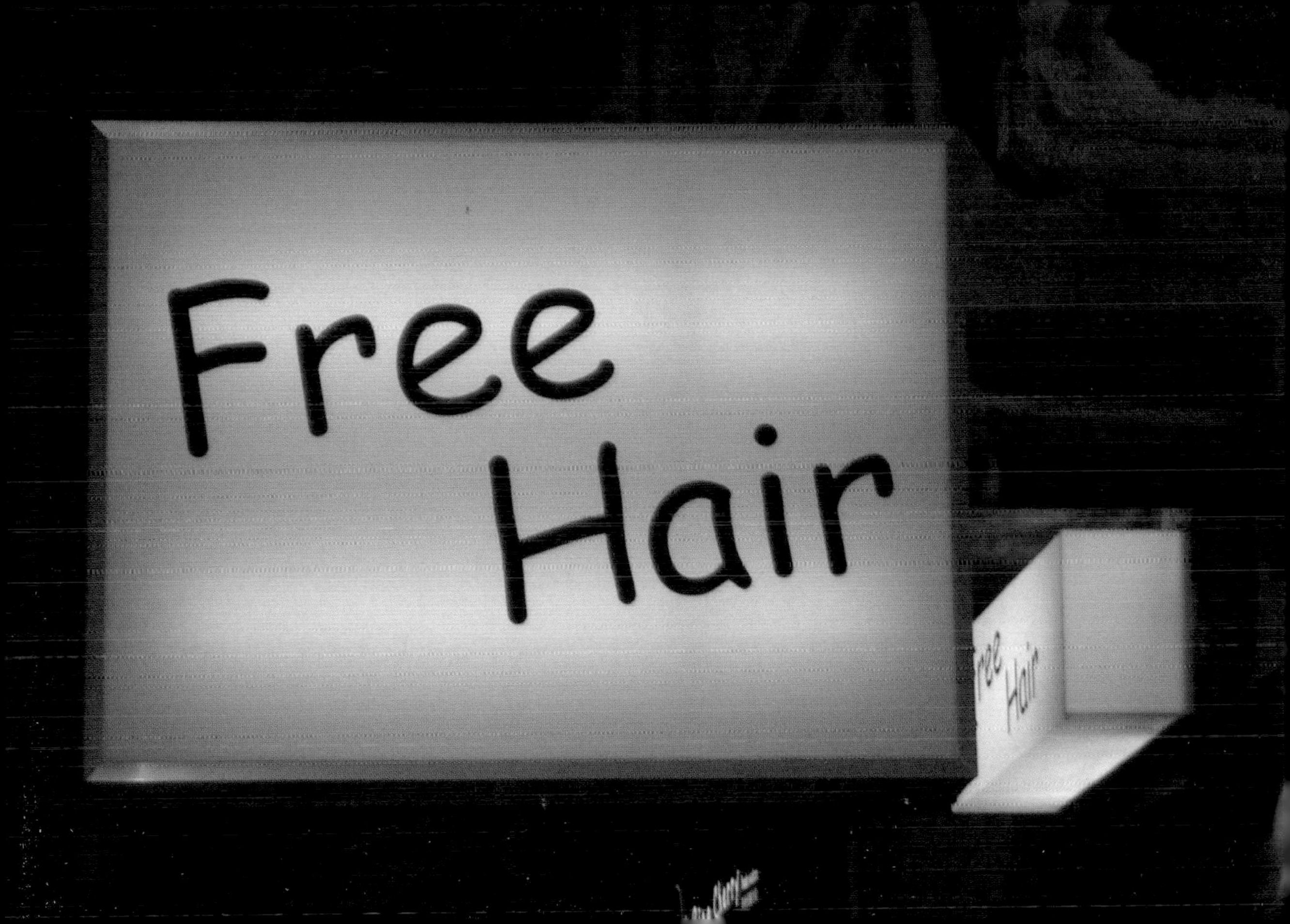
Free
Hair

THE COUNTRYSIDE

Things can take many a strange twist out in the sticks. Don't be fooled by the fresh country air, or those adorable gambolling lambs. Beneath all that serenity lie fertile pastures for tickled funny bones – especially if you have an eye for a bucolic oddity, as many *Telegraph* readers do.

Would you, for example, expect to encounter a playful sense of irony in rural Alaska? One reader found it in a bullet-ridden 'no target shooting' sign.

The refrigeration-van man, marooned in the icy Canadian wilderness, was perhaps unaware of the irony of his own situation – or of the snapper lurking behind a snow drift.

And did the sign-makers for the Ocean View Trail turn-off twig that their work – which highlighted the lack of an ocean view – might raise an eyebrow or two?

Linguistic quirks also stand out. Take the Lake District sign asking for caution when approaching livestock: 'Tek care, lamb ont road'; you can practically hear the writer's Cumbrian vowels – or is that just the sound of someone's tongue lodging in their cheek?

Then there's the one about the Irish village shopkeeper who wants you to go back to the back if you have the front to go to the front. Or something.

And spare a thought for the Czech contributor who used to wonder why so many tourists slowed down to take pictures of her village's welcome sign. Only after she moved away from the small community of Horní Police to learn English did she find out.

DEAD END →
Location: Sutton Hoo ancient burial site, Suffolk, UK
Spotted by: Paul Smith

← **MAGICAL MYSTERY TOUR**
Location: Beijing, China
Spotted by: Ian Gibson

↑ **LEAF IT OUT**
Location: San Francisco, USA
Spotted by: Huw Griffiths

← **JURASSIC PATH**
Location: Devon, UK
Spotted by: Christina Hunt

→ **KWIK GIT**
Location: France
Spotted by: Mike Cartlidge

→ **ECKY THUMP**
Location: Lake District, UK
Spotted by: David Thomson

→ **BACK TO FRONT**
Location: Kinsale, Ireland
Spotted by: Stuart Milne

← **ESCAPE TO THE OUTDOORS**
Location: South Africa
Spotted by: Clint Pavkovich

← **LEAP OF FAITH**
Location: Látrabjarg, Iceland
Spotted by: Dr Jim Reynolds

→ **EASY TARGET**
Location: Alaska, USA
Spotted by: Patricia Ewing

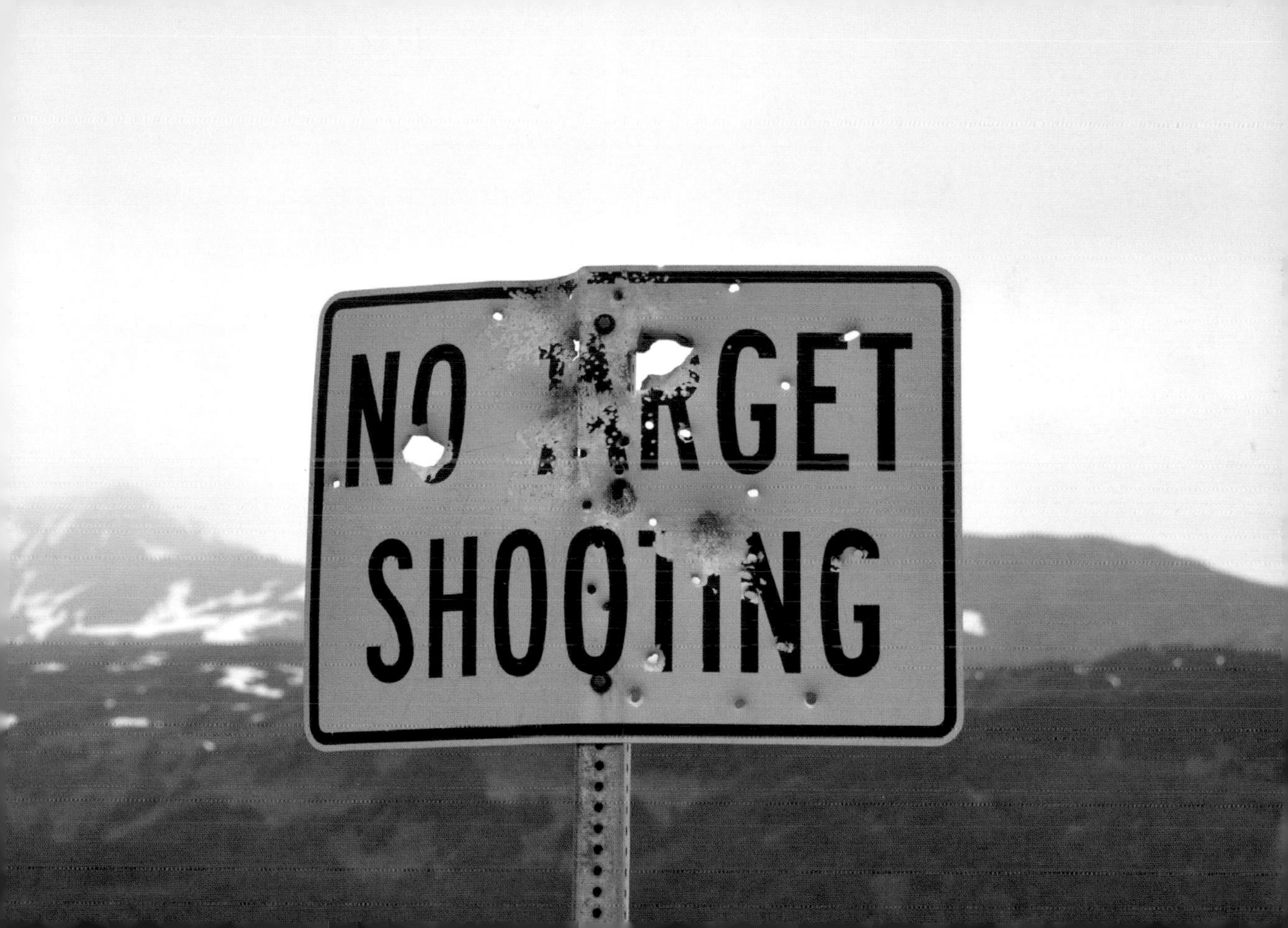
NO TARGET
SHOOTING

← DEAD AND BURIED
Location: Australia
Spotted by: Ron Baker

↑ BUTTS IN BLOOM
Location: Butts County,
Georgia, USA
Spotted by: Thomas Cole

↑ FISHERMAN'S FRIEND
Location: Norfolk, UK
Spotted by: Hazel Aslett

← **DEEP FREEZE**
Location: near Lake Louise, Canada
Spotted by: John Ryall

→ **ALLSORTS**
Location: Tasmania
Spotted by: Dr Robin Hendy

→ **LIEUTENANT OF LOVE**
Location: Czech Republic
Spotted by: Helena

→ **MEMBERS ONLY**
Location: California, USA
Spotted by: Michael Rolfe

← **KEEPING SANITY
LOCKED AWAY**
Location: Nottinghamshire, UK
Spotted by: Leigh Pienaar

ANIMALS

Never work with animals, the comedian W C Fields once advised his show-business pals – and here are a few clues why.

Take the belligerent pigeon perched on a sign for a birds-only wetland sanctuary; the cow munching blithely by a 'no grazing' board; and the rooster strutting purposefully towards a Cayman Islands' KFC ('We do chicken right'). As Mr Fields suggested, you can never quite trust members of the animal kingdom to behave properly.

Mind you, sign-makers' efforts are not always entirely appropriate themselves. It takes a certain perverse sort to advertise the delights of petting little bunnies at 'Rabbit Fun Land', and then to flag up the culinary delights of rabbit satay – on the very same billboard.

A similarly twisted marketing philosophy seems to have been adopted by a Wyoming taxidermist, proudly advertising its stuffed animals as 'Wildlife in natural habitat'.

Over the next pages, you will find dung beetles given the right of way over everything else in Africa; a South Dakotan dog so strange it requires a warning sign; and an Indian zoo that manages to find eighteen different ways of asking people to leave its animals alone.

As for the Florida wildlife park's sign requesting onlookers not to 'molest' the alligators … well, do they really need to ask?

IF YOUR NAME'S NOT DOWN, → YOU'RE NOT COMING IN
Location: Slimbridge Wetlands Centre, Gloucestershire, UK
Spotted by: Estelle Manson-Whitton

Selamat Datang Ke

Rabbit Fun Land

Petting Zone

Rabbit Satay

www.earcsb.com 012-636 2833
012-672 8839

TAMAN ARNAB DESTINASI TERUNGGUL
TUMPUAN KELUARGA DI BANDAR KAJANG

→ **GATOR HATERS**
Location: Pinellas Park, Florida, USA
Spotted by: Stephen LeBlanc

→ **DON'T HAVE A COW**
Location: unknown
Spotted by: Sheira Pullin

← **BUNNY OLD WORLD**
Location: Unspecified
Spotted by: Gene and Melanie George

↑ THANAKS FOR READING
Location: Taiwan
Spotted by: Simon Penny

**↑ USE THE WHEELIE
BINS PROVIDED**
Location: Malta
Spotted by: Len Hyams

**→ BESIDES MY MISSING LEG,
YOU MEAN?**
Location: New Territories,
Hong Kong
Spotted by: Mike Fielding and
Mary Hayden

防鯊網已於 <u>2009 年 11 月 5 日</u>拆除，以便維修。不便之處，敬請原諒。

The shark prevention net was dismantled for maintenance on <u>5/11/2009</u>. We apologize for any inconvenience caused.

CHICKENS
KEEP
DOGS ON
LEAD

→ **WONKY DONKEY**
Location: London, UK
Spotted by: Kiera Davidson

→ **FUNNY FIDO**
Location: South Dakota, USA
Spotted by: Peter Holme

← **AND NO FOWLING**
Location: Somerset, UK
Spotted by: Kay Bagon

THIS ENCLOSURE SPONSORED BY FREE THE BEARS FUND INC.

www.freethebears.org.au

→ **NEVER MIND THE ELEPHANTS**
Location: Addo Elephant Park, South Africa
Spotted by: Nicholas Fry

→ **DON'T GET THE HUMP**
Location: Bahrain
Spotted by: Mal Girling

← **BEARLY BELIEVABLE**
Location: Edinburgh, UK
Spotted by: Charlotte Sevil

↑ FEARLESS CHICKEN
Location: Cayman Islands
Spotted by: Kirsty Griffiths

Flag – Blue Flag – Blaue Flagg
DK – 2450 København SV
Telefon +45 33 79 09 79
Email: bf@friluftsraadet.dk
www.blaaflag.dk

Fang en krabbe
Nogen synes at en krabbe er ulækker. Andre synes at den er sjov og spændende. Krabben er ikke farlig selvom den kan se meget grum ud. Den kan højst nappe dig lidt, men den kan ikke nå dig med klosaksene, hvis du tager den ovenfra med en finger på hver side af skjoldet.

Catch a crab
Some people think that a crap is disgusting. Other thinks that the crap is fun and exciting. The crab is not dangerous even though it looks nasty. It can bite you a bit, but not if you hold on to the shield from the top.

Fang mal eine Krabbe
Einige finden eine Krabbe ekelhaft. Andere finden sie lustig und spannend. Die Krabbe ist nicht gefährlich, obwohl sie so aussehen kann. Sie kann höchstens schnappen, aber sie kann dich nicht mit der Scheren schaden, wenn du die von oben auf den Schild nimmst.

Forberedelser	1. Preparation	1. Vorbereitungen
gle små stykker fisk eller	Get some small pieces of fish or mussels.	Kleine Stückchen Fisch oder Muschel schaffen
nor fast om en klemme. pand eller et akvarium sted, hvor du kan begynde	Tie a line to a clothes-peg. Find a bucket or an aquarium. Find a good spot for fishing on a marina or a jetty.	Eine Schnüre an eine Klammer binden. Einen Eimer oder ein Aquarium herbeischaffen. Eine Stelle zum Angeln im Hafen oder von einem Badesteg finden.
m regel godt at gøre på en r fra en badebro. nings vest på en havn.	Remember to wear lifejacket on a marina.	Rettungsweste im Hafen nicht vergessen.

↑ TALKING CRAB
Location: Denmark
Spotted by: Nick Coleman

→ WHEN IS LUNCH AGAIN?
Location: Bourton-on-the-Water, UK
Spotted by: Mark Hacker

PENGUIN
FEEDING
TIMES

2·30 pm

Our readers are a lovely bunch: intelligent, well-travelled and, as *Sign Language* attests, capable of spotting an amusing opportunity for wordplay at 100 paces. But this keen sense of humour takes on any number of forms, from the admirably highbrow to the downright saucy.

Channelling our inner adolescents for the purposes of compiling this book was far easier than it should have been. We often found ourselves sniggering and nudging each other when a particularly rude photo had been submitted. We tittered at unconventional family planning advice ('use rear entrance' seems to be a popular sign outside clinics). We chuckled at the Australian builder whose company Viagra Fencing promised erections his customers could only dream of.

And we blushed when we consulted a dictionary to discover just exactly what a merkin is.

What follows are the funniest, and smuttiest, signs we could persuade our moral betters to publish.

Any deemed too shocking for the bookshops have been banished to the office archives. Those of a prudish disposition should look away now.

PRIVATE PROPERTY →
Location: Hanoi, Vietnam
Spotted by: Jonathan Davies

TRY

COCK

TODAY

PLEASE

船底観覧室入口
BOTTOM SIGHT-SEEING ROOM

← REAR VIEW
Location: Aquarium in
Shimoda, Japan
Spotted by: Simon Enstone

↑ SATISFACTION GUARANTEED
Location: Australia
Spotted by: Brian Samson

↑ COME HERE OFTEN?
Location: Perth, Australia
Spotted by: Peter Hobbs

← LADIES' FAVOURITE
Location: Greece
Spotted by: Simon Peakman

→ THEY'RE THE DOG'S
Location: Indiana, USA
Spotted by: Glyn Garside

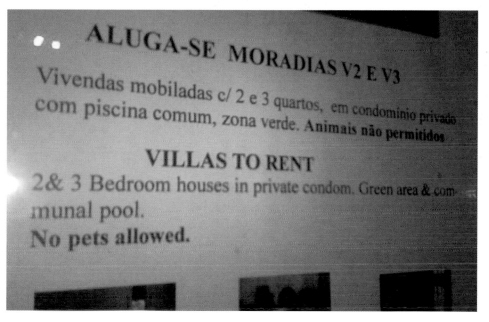

← CUP AND SAUCY
Location: Barmouth, Wales,
Spotted by: David Bremner

↑ STEER CLEAR OF THE COMMUNAL POOL
Location: Almancil, Portugal
Spotted by: 'Tom'

↑ **BOTTOM-OF-THE-RANGE
FIREWORKS**
Location: Barcelona, Spain
Spotted by: Graham Weeks

→ **HIGH RISE**
Location: Jubail, Saudi Arabia
Spotted by: Colum Cantillon

Net: 130g

The plant volatile oil rapidly seeps the whole body flesh, promotes the whole body blood circulatio the affable cerebrum and the muscle, eliminate wearily, the temperate pure flesh, simultaneously moistens the flesh, to the gentleman premature ejaculation, the sexual impotence, the sexual intercourse excessively are many, lacks the ability to do what one would like, lifts but the firmness to have good preventing and controlling and the treatment result.

Application method: After first uses the lukewarm water fully to be moist the skin, repeatedly cl with the scented soap, causes the volatile oil by the skin full absorption, the back water flushing

← A BURNING DESIRE TO GO
Location: Languedoc, France
Spotted by: Marion Webster

↑ FOOL-PROOF
Location: Packet of 'Man Sex Fancy Soap' in Dar Es Salaam, Tanzania
Spotted by: Fred Saugman

← **UNDIE ORDERS**
Location: Dry cleaners in Alliance, Ohio, USA
Spotted by: Stephen LeBlanc

← **STOP MERKIN ME LAUGH**
Location: Argentina
Spotted by: Paul Manning

→ **HOLY MOLEY**
Location: France
Spotted by: Andy and Sue Chamberlain

→ SIGHT FOR SORE EYES
Location: Chester-le-Street
Leisure Centre, UK
Spotted by: Darren Worthy

← SEX DRIVE
Location: Diksmuide, Belgium
Spotted by: Judy McGinnis

↑ PRICES ARE STIFF
Location: Trader Jack's restaurant,
Rarotonga, Cook Islands

← HEAPS OF GOODNESS
Location: Serbia
Spotted by: Pauline Allsop

**→ PETER'S BROTHER,
THE UNDERWEAR SALESMAN**
Location: Virginia, USA
Spotted by: David Jacobs

Cube # 13411

G. Stringfellow

→ NETHER NETHER LAND
Location: Chessington World
of Adventures, UK
Spotted by: Tony Peters

← TASTES LIKE CHICKEN
Location: Swindon, UK
Spotted by: L Mills

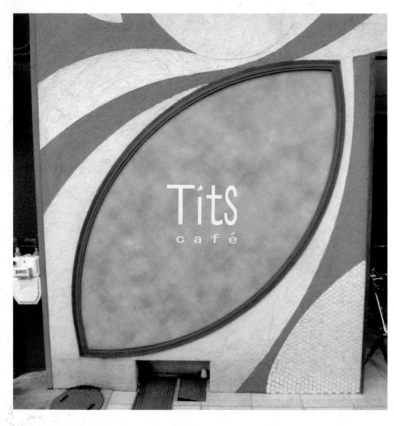

← ONE OF A PAIR
Location: Kyoto, Japan
Spotted by: Ben Janssens

→ HAIR CONDITIONING
COMES AS STANDARD
Location: Marbella, Spain
Spotted by: Matt James

← **BAPS**
Location: France
Spotted by:
Andy and Sue
Chamberlain